T0161748

THE DISCARDED LIFE

THE DISCARDED LIFE

poems

Adam Kirsch

Red Hen Press | *Pasadena, CA*

Book design by Mark E. Cull

Library of Congress Cataloging-in-Publication Data

Names: Kirsch, Adam, 1976– author.
Title: The discarded life: poems / Adam Kirsch.
Description: First edition. | Pasadena, CA: Red Hen Press, [2022]
Identifiers: LCCN 2021043197 (print) | LCCN 2021043198 (ebook) | ISBN
   9781636280158 (trade paperback) | ISBN 9781636280165 (epub)
Subjects: LCSH: Coming of age—Poetry. | LCGFT: Poetry.
Classification: LCC PS3611.I77 D57 2022 (print) | LCC PS3611.I77 (ebook)
   | DDC 811/.6—dc23
LC record available at https://lccn.loc.gov/2021043197
LC ebook record available at https://lccn.loc.gov/2021043198

The National Endowment for the Arts, the Los Angeles County Arts Commission,
the Ahmanson Foundation, the Dwight Stuart Youth Fund, the Max Factor Family
Foundation, the Pasadena Tournament of Roses Foundation, the Pasadena Arts &
Culture Commission and the City of Pasadena Cultural Affairs Division, the City
of Los Angeles Department of Cultural Affairs, the Audrey & Sydney Irmas Chari-
table Foundation, the Meta & George Rosenberg Foundation, the Albert and Elaine
Borchard Foundation, the Adams Family Foundation, Amazon Literary Partnership,
the Sam Francis Foundation, and the Mara W. Breech Foundation partially support
Red Hen Press.

First Edition
Published by Red Hen Press
www.redhen.org

To Remy

1.

It used to be that everything that happened—
The things I did and that were done to me,
The faces and the places and the names—
Glowed with an almost infinite importance;
The texture of events was rough with meaning,
Helping the memory to cling to them.
Whether it is the endless pawing over
Of a few old mementoes of the mind
That makes them cool and slacken to the touch,
Or whether life begins to reveal itself,
As nothing but a choose-your-own-adventure
That leads us by a billion different paths
To the same landmarks and the same conclusion,
Eventually the past begins to leak
The meanings that I took such pains to store there.
I feel it happening, the way that HAL
Could feel the slow dismantling of his mind.
If now's the time, before I age into
The wisdom or indifference of detachment,
To write down something of the way it happened,
It's not because the circumstances matter,
But that the soul of meaning can't survive
Outside the body of contingency.

2.

In the beginning, I am holding hands
With someone who has been erased completely,
Except that I believe it was a woman,
Whom inference has turned into a nurse;
In this way, probability fills in
The blanks the mind should not apologize
For leaving, since the details of her name,
Appearance, what she said and did, could not
Have mattered less to me at two years old,
Watching the closing elevator doors
That left me, for the first time in my life,
On the wrong side, the side without my parents.
What happened next has also been erased,
Until I seem to find myself supine
On a rolling table, being moved from one
Illuminated station to the next,
As a black mask is fitted on my face
And I inhale a sour metallic wind
That scatters me to nothingness again.
So memory begins with an incision;
So memory consists of an incision,
A scar upon oblivion, which gropes
Its own smooth length in unobstructed bliss
Until the sutures of experience
Disturb its touch, demanding explanation,
And consciousness emerges in the cut.

3.

Three Muppets, alternating in a rhyme—
Cat, sat, hat, perhaps, or ball, hall, wall—
Seemed as surprised as I was when a fourth
Darted between them and the camera lens,
Shouting the rhymes that he had taken over
As if they were a war-cry or a curse.
Whatever gentle souls at PBS
Designed the skit or held the Muppet-strings
Would have been shocked to see the way I tore
In sudden terror from the living room,
A categorical, instinctive fear
That had no remedy or explanation,
And wouldn't be repeated till the night,
Years later, when the screen of my Atari,
Normally filled with blocky cars and spaceships,
Vomited up a solid wall of symbols—
Hashmarks, exclamations, ampersands—
My brain could not decode or tolerate.
If nothing's been as terrifying since,
Perhaps I owe it to those early glitches
That taught me how to apprehend the form
Disaster takes, the sudden rushing-up
Of something that is not supposed to be.

4.

The death of Mr. Hooper doesn't need
A footnote for the fleeting demographic
That came of age in 1983,
Crying or trying not to cry as Gordon
Initiated Big Bird in the meaning
Of never coming back. And if the name
Means nothing to our slightly older sisters,
Already jaded by *The Facts of Life*,
Or to the younger brothers who would make
A purple dinosaur their avatar,
Does that mean Mr. Hooper died in vain?
The half-life of a narrative has shrunk;
The jealousy that for millennia
Made every village's absconding wife
Into a Helen, and her paramour
A shrunken Paris, now must find a new
Objective correlative in every decade:
Liz and Eddie Fisher, Brad and Angie,
Or what new pair of illegitimate
And thrilling lovers I have grown too old
To know the famous names of. What is lost
In permanence and dignity—the sense
Of archetypes recycling endlessly,
In which our little lives participate—
Is compensated, maybe, by the love
Of every cohort for its fleeting symbols,
A generation's private names and jokes,
Which start out and end up as trivia
But, in their brief intense significance,

Remind us of our cherishable selves.
Around 2060, when the last
Of Mr. Hooper's mourners will be mourned,
He'll die the second death that lies in wait
For famous men on Wikipedia—
A symbol now degraded to a fact,
Which is a symbol no one's left to love.

5.

I woke up in a room that wasn't mine
To find my father missing. All at once
A possibility revealed itself,
One that I'd been guarded from so well
I didn't even know that it existed:
Having to navigate the world alone.
The need to face a problem like the ones
A hero deals with in a fairy tale
Did not make me heroic; in a gush
Of terror and adrenaline, I ran
Out of the cabin where we'd spent the night,
And raced at random up a grassy hill
To find him calmly looking at the sunrise,
Probably less than fifty feet away.
It is the finding out about the world,
The things of which it's capable, that carves
Such early moments deep into the cortex,
Less like memories than revelations
We spend a lifetime trying to interpret.
What I was shown that morning, I've believed
Since kindergarten, was my nothingness,
The way that loss could make me disappear;
It's only now that it occurs to me
I might have told myself another story:
I learned that the extremity of fear
Is what the tales call courage. After all,
That thirty-second journey up the hill
Was the first quest I ever undertook;
And didn't I return victorious,
My world restored, my bare feet bleeding dew?

6.

That night I went to bed as usual
At eight o'clock, the day already done
For me and so, I thought, for all the world,
Which had no need of going on existing
Without me there to notice it. An hour
Or less had passed when something woke me up—
The Buddy Holly on the stereo,
The unfamiliar sting of cigarettes—
To find our small apartment full of strangers
Who laughed and cooed at me when I emerged,
Trailing a yellow blanket, from my bedroom
Into the unpredictability
And sordid volume of a grown-up party,
Less startled than voluptuously shamed
To find my parents had this secret life
To which I was irrelevant, or worse.
And could it be that if I stayed asleep
That night, when I was five or six years old,
I would have grown into a different person?
Such early traumas aren't accidental,
But revelations and emergences
Of selves that we will never not inhabit;
I'd recognize that shame when it returned,
Much later, being cheated on and dumped
By someone who had also seen the truth
I'd learned so early and could not deny,
That life was more enjoyable without me.

7.

Sex was the secret music tried to tell,
At least the kind of video I saw
Running in gaudy loops on MTV
All evening at my babysitter's house;
In the sarcastic crack of Devo's whips,
The neon leotards of "Physical,"
I sensed a power that I couldn't name
But knew would like to overturn the world
That I could barely manage right side up.
The music I took refuge in was different,
Once I discovered it: Beethoven's Fifth,
One of the first CDs my parents bought,
Began as tedious, prestigious noise
But after many tries I learned to follow
Sound the way I followed thought and speech:
Statement and development and coda,
Turbulent but under strict control,
The way I hoped that I would always be.
It's only now that I can hear the songs
I fled back then with something like affection
For their antique transgressiveness, which sounds
As innocent as I was when I thought
The body and its passion for disorder
Were things I could decide I would ignore.

8.

The curtains at the Miramar Hotel—
Before they were recycled or destroyed
Along with cabins, playgrounds, dining hall,
And all the apparatus that survives
Nowhere but in the senses' memory—
Stored odors that you probably could find
Wherever a sun-saturated fabric
Collected dust, unwashed till summer's end,
But that I've never reencountered elsewhere,
Or wanted to. Those grateful inhalations,
Rituals of arrival, ushered in
The moderate derangement of the senses
That Santa Barbara stood for—just an hour
From home, but an experimental life,
Where breakfast was a fun-size Froot Loops box
Selected from the eight-box travel pack
Of cereals we never bought at home,
And night drives on such unfamiliar streets
It seemed we had gone missing from ourselves.
Do details matter? Does the qualitative
Strangeness of that segment of existence
Live in the metal scent of railroad tracks
Along the beach, on which a penny, placed
At the right moment, would be flattened out
To a featureless memento of brute force?
Today, the melodrama of the last
Goodbye to Miramar, which at the time
Seemed the poetic acme of nostalgia—
Suffering borrowed from a future self
That would recall the curtains with a sigh—

No longer interests me; I can't afford it.
What matters now is what is usable:
The need for periodic alternation,
Like school and summer, city and the beach,
To mitigate the staleness of the sameness
That saturates me everywhere I go.

9.

The wooden box I built and painted white
Would soon acquire a vinegary smell
I couldn't yet identify as beer,
The beer itself remaining just a rumor
Vaguely attached to what I cared about:
The bottle caps that I spent years collecting.
Where did I find them? No one drank at home,
Which made me more resourceful: on the beach,
On sidewalk corners, by recycling bins,
The treasures waited, precious though discarded,
To serve the child's and the collector's passion
For delegating their identity.
Buds and Miller Lites were everywhere,
But sometimes you would find a German name,
Much rarer then than now: a Michelob,
A Lowenbrau with lion's body rampant,
A Heineken with red, five-pointed star.
How did the names imply the images?
There had to be a logic, which remained
More powerful for being so uncertain;
Like heraldry or Kabbalistic symbols,
The bottle caps were emblems of a world
Endlessly rich in meanings and in kinds,
Whose trash itself felt more to me like wealth
Than all the money I have hoarded since.

10.

The last fumes of the sixties lingered on
Inside the prefab walls of Wildwood School,
Where posters urging "Yes on ERA"
Beamed cheerfully as children bearing names
Like Bodhi, Star, and Rainbow shuffled in
To start the day with union marching-songs
And chanteys praising the endangered whales.
If even here we knew about aggression,
If boys loved breaking one another's arms
In wrestling matches in the asphalt yard
(A cast or two per classroom was the norm)
And one, the most ingenious, ran a scam
Convincing me that if I didn't hand
My *Star Wars* action figures over, he
Would find and kill my parents—which I did
For weeks, in fear of his omnipotence—
The fault was not the teachers', whom we knew
By first name only; no one ever scrawled it
On the tabula rasa of our minds;
We must have brought it with us, like a lunchbox.
Conveniently, I can't remember what
I did or said, or who the victim was,
The time the teacher brought us face to face
And coaxed me gently to apologize:
All I remember is the liberation
Of realizing that I didn't need
To *mean* it when I said that I was sorry—
That I could feel resentment, not remorse,
And no one else would know it. What I learned
Of Hopi customs and kachina dolls

Lies, like the school itself, in disrepair,
Except for that day's inadvertent lesson:
Good is what we have to seem to be,
Not something anybody ever is.

11.

The morning meeting, usually a time
For singing labor hymns and protest songs,
Was wrong from the beginning. Teachers stood
With stricken faces, and the principal
Could not stop crying even as she took
The stage to say that Julian had died.
No one, apparently, was bold enough
To stop his mother as she seized the mic,
Watery in a fog of Valium,
And told us how he'd woken up last night
To tell her the first portion of a dream
Whose end he'd promised to confide this morning,
When she had found him on his pillow, dead.
As though she had forgotten that the horror
Of casual and causeless interruption
Is something that adults must try to keep
A secret for as long as possible,
Like Santa's nonexistence. Later on,
A patch of garden named for Julian
Was planted in the schoolyard, with a plaque
That meant a little less with every year,
Until a generation came that knew
Nothing of him except that he had gone
So far ahead of all the rest of us
That even now we haven't quite caught up.

12.

A missile with Cyrillic characters
Hung in the air above Los Angeles,
Seconds from consummating what I knew
Was coming long before I saw the show—
The color remake of the Twilight Zone,
An episode I dreamed about for years:
A woman had the power to make time stop
Though she could never start it up again
Now that the warhead was about to hit.
We lived inside that moment of delay,
Knowing the impact couldn't be avoided:
In *WarGames*, *The Day After*, *On the Beach*,
We gave ourselves a foretaste of extinction,
Its sweet dread and acidic vertigo.
I hoped that it would come when I was sleeping:
The flash, and then, before I had a chance
To notice that the sun was up at night,
The shockwave that would turn me into ash,
A prone stain on a wall or comforter,
Like in the photographs from Hiroshima.
From time to time, a child would make the news
For writing letters to the President,
Explaining that she wanted to grow up,
Begging him not to end the world too soon.
How could he make her understand that no one,
Not Reagan nor Andropov, was in charge
Of all the bristling MIRVs and Minutemen;
They were the servants of a deeper logic
Which says that everything that is potential

Comes to be actual eventually,
And everything that has to happen happens.
It's strange to think it hasn't happened yet.

13.

The most of winter that we ever knew
Was a gray, cloudy tincture of the air,
The minor chill of fifty-five degrees,
The sense of something coming to an end.
Was it a premonition of December,
The slope of asphalt as I walked to class
Making a lonely angle with the sky,
Or was it nothing you could name at all,
Just an inscrutable synaptic lapse,
That makes that day when I was ten years old
Seem to me now an entry point or foretaste
Of devastated atmospheres to come?
The knowledge of how everything can lessen,
How all at once intention and desire
Can fade and leave you no coordinates
By which to plot your motion through the world,
Felt to me at first like being homesick,
Which I beguiled by singing to myself
The mellow pop of 1986,
Until eventually the world returned
As I still trusted that it always would—
As certainly as the withdrawing tide
Comes hurrying to cover up the wrack
And filth it momentarily exposed,
The ground that we were never meant to see,
Much less to spend a lifetime dwelling on.

14.

School is a place where nothing's meant to happen,
Which made that morning's bulletin historic
For being broadcast right inside the classroom;
They must have thought us old enough to learn
That history is something going wrong,
The shuttle torn into a Y of a smoke
While Houston kept on sending messages
As though they couldn't see what we were seeing.
At the assembly where the principal
Informed us what was natural to feel,
The jokes began already: what did Christa
Say to her husband just before the launch?
What color were her eyes? The biggest shock
Was not what happened, but the ruthless speed
With which the big kids turned it into punchlines
So perfect, so hilarious with malice:
Was anyone our age so cynical?
I was too young to understand the wisdom
Of that instinctive hardening of heart
In self-defense against the kind of world
Where it was clear that no one was in charge,
Where even heroes did their best and failed,
And Christa's blue eyes turned to food for fish.

15.

The dungeon I explored in *Wizardry*
Was nothing more than lines and polygons,
All that the bulky monochrome display
Could generate from five-inch floppy disks
You had to keep inserting and withdrawing,
Like turning hand cranks on an early Ford.
The lines defined a labyrinth of rooms
And corridors you couldn't hope to track
Without a sheet of graphing paper; so
I diligently drew myself a map,
Noting the spot where suddenly an orc
Would show himself and make my avatars,
The mages, bards, and dagger-wielding thieves,
Engage in battles that were nothing more
Than numbers generated randomly
To calculate the damages in hit points,
As if the Apple IIe CPU
Were just a souped-up twenty-sided die.
How many hours were made to disappear
In vacant quests whose actual reward
Was a transported singlemindedness—
My room illuminated by the green
Flicker of pixels from that other realm
Where death was canceled by a quick reload,
And every maze was small enough to master?

16.

The Big One, topping out the Richter scale,
Was something no one ever could forget
Or really pay attention to, like death.
All the half-hearted drills and preparations—
The closet full of flashlights and canned soup,
Diving for cover under plastic desks,
Avoiding windows that were sure to blow
To jagged shrapnel when the moment came—
Were less like preparation than appeasement,
As though the Big One would be satisfied
By all these recognitions of its power
And not be tempted to a demonstration,
Beyond the rattling of our locker doors
Or tearing of a chalkboard from the wall.
If it were not for the occasional
Report from Sylmar, Northridge, or some other
Place you didn't know existed till
It didn't any longer, you might think
The San Andreas was a teaching tool
Like Scantrons or the overhead projector—
A fiction meant to inculcate the skill
That we would end up needing most of all,
Of living only tentatively in
A world whose timer is already set.

17.

The lens flare that defines the seventies
In movies like *McCabe and Mrs. Miller*
Was not a fad; the world was like that then,
Glaring and grainy in the memory
As in the canisters of brittle film
Projected at the Beverly or Aero,
Revival houses that cannot revive
The angel city that I used to live in.
Before the malls went up and were torn down,
Before the Grove and Third Street Promenade
Seceded from the city to afford
A stylish sanctuary to the rich
Where they could visit Anthropologie
Without the fear of getting asked for change,
A Saturday meant browsing Westwood Village,
Its five competing bookshops, used and new,
And always leaving time for the arcade
Where I would shovel quarters in Galaga.
This was the long interregnum of freeways,
After the Red Car trolleys were removed
And long before the building of the subway,
When going anywhere involved an hour
Of sitting in companionable traffic
Whose idling roar and smell of burning gas
Combined to make my childhood's microclimate,
Which better mufflers and improved A/C
Have rendered as outmoded as the smog
The bowl of mountains disappeared beneath
Each summer in a brown polluted smudge,
Which you could smell and taste on certain days

When the alert went out to stay indoors.
Now, when I drive down Wilshire Boulevard,
Its few remaining Googie diners lost
Amid the Coffee Beans and ATMs,
I see the city not as it's become
But as I like to misremember it:
Everything cheaper, dirtier, and better,
Discolored by the streaks of innocence
I must have left behind me when I left.

18.

When nothing's left of my Bar Mitzvah portion
But memories of leprosy and cubits,
And I've forgotten all the names of tropes
And tunes I was laboriously taught
By patient Cantor F., ex-boy-soprano,
Who found a respite from my ignorance
In talking through our lessons on the phone
With old friends who remembered him as Shmuelke,
Star of the *bimah* in his glory days;
When all the laws that were halfheartedly
Transmitted by adults who didn't keep them
But weren't bold enough to let them go
Have almost lost the power to reproach me,
Now that Hashem who once was here and there
And everywhere has shrunk into himself,
Leaving the air more breathable, and colder;
What can I hold onto but the Torah,
Not the commandments but the scroll itself,
Clutching it in my arms on Yom Kippur
Like an enormous, velvet-swaddled baby
That everybody wants to pet and kiss
As I parade it through the congregation
With just a little less self-consciousness
Than on the day when I became a man
By promising I wasn't going to drop it.

19.

The German flight attendant couldn't bear
To search the passports of the passengers,
The way the Arab terrorists demanded,
To pick out all the Jews and have them shot.
Raid on Entebbe was the film, I think,
A special evening show at Hebrew school,
Where they of course intended us to learn
A lesson from the Uzi-armed commandos
Who struck at dawn and freed the hostages—
The new Jews who would not await "selection,"
The way our perished relatives had done
In places that composed a litany
We learned as well or better than the Sh'ma.
I still remember the typography
In which the camps were printed, red on black,
On posters that adorned the classroom wall
The way the ghosts of all our enemies
Crowded the lessons and the calendar:
Egyptians, Babylonians, and Romans,
Greeks and Crusaders, Soviets and Nazis.
Unfair, of course, to focus on the fears
They gave us and ignore the many gifts;
So why is it the fears that I remember?
Perhaps the answer's simple as it seems:
God's not real, but being murdered is.

20.

It was a joke, a way of showing off:
Anything, I said, could be compared
To anything with just a little forcing.
For instance, God could be compared to hairspray:
Both were invisible but everywhere
At Jewish summer camp where daily prayers
And teased-up bangs were equally in fashion.
I don't think anybody was amused,
But somehow the idea was a clue:
If everything could be a metaphor,
The world must be subordinate to language,
Which meant, to me and what I could come up with.
If I could play with the idea of God,
Who was more godlike? Maybe disbelief
And metaphor are twin discoveries,
Clinging to one another as they plunge
In the abyss of correspondences—
Unless it is the God in everything
That makes the possibility of likeness,
In which case likening is not a game
But something like a tribute or a prayer,
An effort to decode the signature
The world would be, if only we could read it.

21.

Sitting by the stereo in headphones,
Browsing through the pile of old LPs
I rescued from a never-opened closet,
I gave myself the doubtful education
That opera offers, and that moralists
Had warned against for generations, till
The later styles of musical rebellion
Made arias sound as innocent as culture.
Because I didn't know this, I knew better;
From prostitutes and libertines, I learned
The secret of the sweetness of transgression.
Love, which I had thought was purely good—
Benevolent and matrimonial—
Now showed its other faces: Violetta's
Orgasmic hymns to folly and desire,
"Delight and cross" of the reluctant heart;
Donna Elvira's joy in her abjection,
In being dumped and used and dumped again.
Was this what Mrs. Brown had meant to teach
That afternoon when, bored or unprepared,
She played the class a tape of *Amadeus*,
A missionary for the higher things?
The lesson took, but not as she intended:
The high is nothing but the lowest, turned
Into a kind of decorous abstraction,
A voice distended with perversity,
The melting tone of something giving way.

22.

A neighborhood, to almost everyone,
Is "good" when there is nothing going on
Nearby to which you have to pay attention.
For me, now, too; but not at age fifteen,
Pacing the lawns and gutters of Mar Vista
In search of signs of something happening,
The life I had concocted out of books
And sexlessness and vacant afternoons.
How could I hope to find it where the streets
Were built without a sidewalk as a sign
There wasn't any point in going further?
More likely, life was in the coffee shops
Whose off-key and insinuating names—
The Bourgeois Pig and Van Gogh's Ear—had come
Like rumors from remotest Hollywood,
But which I didn't think I was equipped
To patronize, not knowing how to act
Among the college-age aristocrats
Who held court over cups of cappuccino.
I knew to get from where I was to there
Would take more than the car I didn't have;
It needed the ability to talk
To girls I hadn't known since second grade,
To linger with a cigarette and book,
To order cappuccinos and to like them;
I'd know that life was happening at last
When I became a person who could sit
In Van Gogh's Ear and look like I belonged.

23.

The first night, we were rousted from our bunks
And sent to huddle in a grassy field
Out of the path of the approaching fires,
Whose red smoke drifted close enough to make
Our eyes burn like the chaparral around us,
As small planes circled, dumping loads of foam.
If camp had welcomed us another way,
Would what was slowly drying out inside me
Have turned to ash so quickly? Right away,
I knew that there was something going wrong:
At first it felt like wanting to go home,
But daily deepened into something worse,
A feeling that I couldn't have imagined
And now believed I never wouldn't feel.
Home wouldn't fix it. Everything was gone:
Not only happiness, which comes and goes
Like the systolic rhythm of the tide,
But even the idea of happiness,
Which seemed remote and irretrievable
Like something that I hadn't thought to pack
In the green duffel bag from army surplus.
How could time pass at all inside a world
Where I'd forgotten what it meant to want?
Of course, the weeks went by; but on the bus
That took us home I knew it wasn't over,
That brains like bones can never fully mend
Once they've discovered they are breakable;
There is a part of me immune to time,
Still stuck back there and motioning for help
In the dark glare of the approaching burn.

24.

"We'll pound those camel-fuckers into sand,"
A drunk beside the bar was bellowing,
As if he somehow hadn't been informed
This was to be a different kind of war
Whose weapons would be flags and yellow ribbons
And signs declaring "we support the troops."
The build-up, like the marketing campaign
For *Batman* that took place the year before,
Was more impressive than the main event;
The many weeks of watching senators
Debate the New World Order on TV
Made me believe the war was going to last
At least till I was old enough to fight it.
Was I more disappointed or relieved
When everything was over in the green
Flash of a barracks blown up in the nightscope,
As burning soldiers fled into the night
Like ants whose nest was doused with gasoline?
Later, a kid who'd taken French with us
Returned in uniform to tell us how
It felt to sit inside a desert tank,
Waiting for the order to advance:
Hot. If there was something more to say,
He didn't think we were prepared to hear it.

25.

One April morning, we woke up to find
The lawn and windshield wearing coats of ash—
The particles of burnt and looted shops
That floated west from Normandie and Florence,
Ignited by the video that played
A dozen times a day on local news,
Bearing its blurry witness to the kicks
And sticks rained down on twitching Rodney King,
Thus answering his question in advance:
There is no way for us to get along.
At school that day, we heard about a bus
Whose driver commandeered it for a tour
Of Compton and South Central, so the kids
Diverted from their Westside journeys home
Would recognize how close the riots were
And learn that innocence can be offensive.
What we took home were other kinds of lessons
That went on proving useful ever since:
The strange effectiveness of boundaries
You won't find listed in the Thomas Guide,
Although the cops are always there to guard them;
The piquancy of waking up to ash
You know will wash off with a garden hose,
A dirty symbol of immunity
From fires that always happen somewhere else.

26.

Google, better than a private eye,
Tracks down my former teachers and reveals
The fates I wished on them have all come true.
Mr. X, who in a purple rage
Once ripped a metal pencil sharpener
Out of the classroom wall where it was bolted
And hurled it at a fleeing ten-year-old;
And Mr. X, who paid me twenty bucks
A week to do his grad-school homework for him,
Until my parents heard and made me stop;
And Mr. X, who waited till the day
Of graduation to begin to sleep
With girls whose grades he'd only just submitted;
And Mrs. X, who showed up drunk to class
And asked for volunteers to cross the street
To buy her beer at the convenience store;
And Mrs. X, who lectured while she smoked
And retailed gossip from the Industry
She picked up in a nightclub after work;
And all the other floridly unfit
Adults who we were told we must respect
Because they were our teachers, now are sick
And wheelchair-bound, or bankrupted, or dead.
Which would be justice, if the same result
Had not come for the ones like Mrs. L,
A bit standoffish in her self-respect,
Who taught us everything we had to know
Of RNA and photosynthesis
And then went home to lead another life
We never heard a single thing about.

27.

I'm sure that I could still retrace the route
The bus took to the multiplex and mall
Down Constellation Boulevard, and find
The corner where, one summer afternoon,
High school behind me, college just ahead,
I felt a surge of possibility
Such as I never knew before or since:
The future was a blank for reinvention,
Four years in which the things I never found
At home—like unselfconsciousness, or else
A self of which I needn't be ashamed—
Would give themselves to me as easily
As courses in a catalog. That stretch
Of pavement seems to me it must contain
Deposits of the future still aglow,
A future that remains pristine because
It never condescended to come true;
If time that has been bypassed isn't past,
It must be somewhere, inaccessible
And always still to come, like happiness.

28.

The palm trees after which the neighborhood
Was named were tall but inconspicuous;
Their thin trunks and attenuated fronds
Did almost nothing to obstruct the broad
Expensive blue so many people came
From all points east to live beneath. At night,
You couldn't even say they disappeared;
The palms avoided such dramatic gestures;
Instead, they took a step politely back
To blend in with a light-polluted sky.
Which may be why, in that first eastern winter,
When I looked up to see the silhouettes
Of stripped black branches spidering across
The deeper blackness of a frozen night,
I seemed to make a promise to myself,
Or else to them, their witchy purity,
Not to forget the message they imparted.
Which was? And what did I believe I owed
To the first holy hush of falling snow,
A blankness that demanded a response,
The way the pink and purple flare of sunset
On the Pacific never seemed to need?
Something to do with being serious,
With cold and challenge and severity—
Melodramatic watchwords of a boy
Whose promises it's not too late to keep.

29.

Mount Auburn Cemetery was the place
I didn't know I had been looking for:
Ranks of inelegant sarcophagi
Guarding their Harvard and New England bones,
The names familiar from the dining halls
And bookshelves—all those Eliots and Lowells.
No better place for an epiphany
Or visitation, as it seemed to me,
Who grew up in a glass and plastic city
Whose monuments had not been built to last;
Here were tradition and authority,
Things I never knew how much I wanted
Until I found their nineteenth-century,
Granitic incarnation, half an hour
Down Brattle Street from my new freshman dorm.
I sat down there among the dead and waited,
And something came—a feeling or a thought,
Something to do with reverence and connection,
Being adopted by a history
I didn't have the pride or common sense
To know would never have accepted me.
Maybe that doesn't matter: past is mute,
We make it read from our invented scripts;
To die is to consent to be a symbol.
But that's what wouldn't come that afternoon:
The words, the lines, the symbols that I knew
Were what I wanted, more than intuitions.
Why did my own experience already
Seem perishable, insignificant,

Without the words to make a poem of it?
Since that day I've never visited
The place again, that scene of my defeat;
Though now I think I could be happy there,
Learning a different kind of inspiration
From the benign indifference of the dead.

30.

With writing, as with other shameful things,
Desire arrived before ability.
In high school I convinced myself to try
Composing with a pen made out of glass
I'd bought and consecrated to the purpose,
Believing that it took a kind of rite
To write; but I could never figure out
The magic words or gestures that would make
Life vanish so that poetry could start.
I failed for years before I understood
The wand was pointed in the wrong direction:
It was myself that had to disappear
For words to start to lumber into motion
In the plain college composition book
I'd taken with me to the coffee shop
That summer night on Venice Boulevard
When something in me caught or slid in place.
Once I began I couldn't think of stopping:
The poem's spell of self-annihilation
Was what I never knew I always needed.
I hardly noticed the withdrawal from life
That went with turning inward and away
As summer lengthened and I stayed indoors,
Missing the trips to *Clueless* and the mall
To write behind the locked door of my room.
If anyone had told me my condition
Would grow till it was irreversible,
I wouldn't have been any more concerned
Than I was by the thought of emphysema
The day I learned to hold a cigarette

With the same fingers that could take a pen
And flick the words like ashes down the page,
Leaving a record of the life consumed.

31.

Because all power is the power to waste,
The thought that every cigarette I smoked
Subtracted minutes—eight or ten, I'd heard—
From the tall, toppling stack of time I owned
Could not discourage me; it just aroused
The gleeful magnanimity a chief
Must feel to see the potlatch treasures go—
To lose all this, and still have more to lose!
Who wouldn't trade the ash-end of existence
For the controlled burn of a summer night,
In a little garden, where the mound of butts
By Labor Day became a monument
To the self-overcoming of the will?
Addiction's an achievement; like belief,
It seems absurd to those who never learned
The habit of impossible assertion,
The excavation of an inner space
For soul to waft and waver in, like smoke.
Still, there's a debt that spirit owes to fact,
Fact that may bide its time, but in the end
Reminds us we don't we live in metaphor,
At least, not in our own; reality
Is plotting constantly, in every cell,
Its squamous, imperturbable revenge.
Like every coward, finally, I quit.

32.

The only education that remains,
When what we learn betrays its uselessness,
Are moments of resistance and defiance,
The counter-pressures that define a self—
My indignation at the great director
Disparaging Trigorin in *The Seagull*,
Declaring him a mediocrity
Because of his reaction to success;
Of all that he had hoped for from his calling—
Fame, contentment, inspiration, love—
Everything proved illusory except
The quiet pleasure of correcting proofs.
Imagine knowing better than Trigorin!
As if there were a life more glamorous
Than disillusioned productivity,
Doing without the need for a belief
In what you're doing. I was on his side;
Here was the possibility of art
Commensurate with being disillusioned
In just the way that I aspired to be—
Art that is nothing else but a devotion
To saying what's unfortunately true.

33.

The campus party was, as usual,
Fueled by one-upmanship and alcohol,
People reduced to standing on their heads
Or issuing outrageous proclamations
To get attention—like the guy whose name
And face I don't remember, but whose words,
Parroted from a classroom and pronounced
With all the dignity of twenty-one,
Seemed marvelous to me at seventeen.
"I call myself a moral perfectionist;
It's my belief that there's a wrong and right
Way to do everything—to cross a room,"
He said, but didn't try to demonstrate
What staggering across a sticky room
With a red plastic beer cup in your hand
Would look like, executed to perfection.
That is what learning is supposed to do,
It seemed to me: to take our arrogance,
The callow yearning never to be wrong,
And turn it into a philosophy,
A code to live by and a phrase to wield.
I haven't yet forgotten. Even now,
When I have ceded almost all of life
To inconvenience and indignity,
And come to terms with what is obvious—
That we invent the notion of perfection
To lend a certain drama to existence,
To turn our lives into a test of skill,
Though no one cares or even pays attention—

Still, there is something in me that believes
That one day I will learn to cross a room
Correctly, and a new life will begin.

34.

Childhood is a long and restless sleep,
The kind of dream you know to be a dream
But can't break free of, though the waking mind
Shrieks an alarm from its imprisonment,
Trying to summon what it knows is out there—
A world of greater clarity and order,
Benevolent because predictable,
The one that grown-ups keep on calling real.
Youth is a waking up in little fits
Of arduously conjured consciousness,
The spirit surging up and falling back
Over and over like a drowning man
Whose lungs keep almost filling up with brine,
Or like a newborn learning how to breathe
The nourishing but insubstantial air
In purple gasps of fury and confusion;
Until at last you find yourself awake,
Dripping and panting on the further shore,
Having evolved successfully to leave
The sea, the womb, the dark, the dream behind,
Which now appear so peaceful in the distance
That it requires an effort to remember
Why it once felt so urgent to escape them.

35.

For very many years, the thought of death
Served as my most effective sedative,
Escorting me to sleep as I rehearsed
How much I wanted and deserved to die.
Now I believe that only the remoteness
And inconceivability of death
Enabled me to yearn for it, the way
His silence is what makes us pray to God;
I needed death to come a little closer,
To swallow it like homeopathy
In tiny doses, self-administered,
Because I recognized instinctively
That only death makes living bearable.
Without it, life's equation doesn't balance
But yields absurdities: a single day's
Ration of failure and humiliation
Would be so huge, so ineffaceable,
That none of us could ever live it down
If we were forced to live with it forever;
Like gravity, our time must be attuned
To just the right proportion if we're not
To be crushed flat or sucked into the void.
Now that I'm old enough for death to be
A thinkable end to any given day,
It doesn't need to be called down so loudly,
With so much inner turmoil and theatrics;
It already surrounds me, like the night
That comes so we will know it's time to sleep.

36.

To say there's nothing I would rather do
Than sleep would be disgraceful. Wouldn't it?
The waking world is always adequate,
Only inadequates think otherwise.
Even if sleep is not exactly death—
A kind of subjectivity remains,
Things happen, though inconsequentially,
Vanishing with the blare of the alarm—
It's close enough to share the nullity
That life is a conspiracy against,
An intricate pretending to ignore;
To say that you would rather be asleep
Is almost wishing you were never born,
The brash illogic of the suicide
Who doesn't understand that, without life,
There is no I to be born or to die,
To suffer or escape from suffering.
The pleasure only lies in the transition,
The luxury of that first hour in bed
As I expand into the knowledge that
Another day has passed without disaster,
At least for me, and that until I wake
I can be sure I won't do something wrong.

37.

The world is watered by a stream of money
That comes and goes in seasons, like the Nile.
It seems so wide at first that you would think
That only fools could fail to get their share;
And yet the banks are always full of crowds
Waving their pails and buckets frantically,
Hoping to shoulder through the competition
And scoop up just enough to fertilize
Their parched, ungiving acre for a season.
A few, the brutal, fortunate, or smart,
Obstruct the flow or engineer canals,
Then bathe in the resulting stagnant pools.
(The weak and sick, of course, don't stand a chance.)
And here and there you'll see a person pause
Amid the anxious pushing of the crowd
To look around him or to watch the sky,
And wonder whether this is what we're born for.
Of course, his problem is he got a sieve
Somehow, when tools were being handed out,
Making him so unfitted for his job
That there is nothing left for him but dreaming.
And all the while, the stream goes rushing past,
Contemptuous, abundant, out of reach.

38.

Why was I born, the old complaint and question,
Does not get answered till you are the one
From whose desire or thoughtlessness is made
Another I who turns to you and asks
Why he was born. The answer must be love,
Dull and unsatisfying as it sounds:
To gratify his parents' urge to love,
The child must be delivered to a world
Whose lovelessness is unendurable.
Perhaps the greatest act of love would be
To leave the child beneath the throne of God,
Unembodied and unhurtable—
To love enough to bear the sacrifice
Of loving someone who remains potential.
Except that something has decreed against it:
The concept of a person can't be loved,
Only the child himself, in front of you,
Real enough to be embraced and damaged.
Still, if the weakness of imagination
Is what ensures we keep on giving birth,
At least we can take comfort in the knowledge
This is a weakness God himself must share:
Why else does he multiply Creation,
Instead of loving the idea of us
And sparing us from the ordeal of being?
God is a father just like every father
Who doesn't love to see his children suffer,
Although they suffer for his need to love.

39.

To say that we do not belong to time
Does not imply that time's escapable,
That after death or in another world
We'll learn to mock at mutability
The way that children scorn the Disney songs
And superheroes they have just outgrown.
I sense it rather in the slow decline
Of my ability to feel regret,
Even as the occasions for regret
Pile up with every day that's forfeited;
Instead of guilt, there comes the certainty
That everything abandoned is postponed,
That all the universe will reconvene,
I don't know how, at some time out of time
To claim at last the quantum of attention
That everything and everyone deserves.
The fact that this will never really happen
Seems not to matter. Whether it's a dream
Or merely an excuse for giving up,
It lingers in its falsehood like a god,
The more consoling for its nonexistence;
For how could we imagine timelessness
Unless there was a part of us that bore
The scar or stigma of eternity?

40.

The pleasure of accumulation pales
Next to the reckless joy of getting rid:
The bonfire of Transformers, G.I. Joes,
And other loot from Hanukkahs gone by,
The adolescent posters stripped from walls
Dotted with pinholes making up a code
Of lost loves and allegiances outgrown,
Until the room approximates a berth
With nothing but a desk, a chair, a bed,
All the equipment needed for a voyage
Away from everything I used to be.
Poetry is a method of disposal,
Giving a decent burial in words
To the discarded life I have no use for—
Or else a way to throw it overboard
As the balloon jerks higher toward the sun,
Affording one last comprehensive view
Of places I will never land again.

BIOGRAPHICAL NOTE

Adam Kirsch is a poet and critic whose writing appears regularly in *The New Yorker* and other publications. He is the author of three previous collections of poetry and several books of criticism and biography, and has received a Guggenheim Fellowship. An editor at the *Wall Street Journal*, he has taught at Columbia University and Sarah Lawrence College. He was born in Los Angeles and now lives in New York City.